W9-CNO-269

# Eye Gunk

## by Grace Hansen

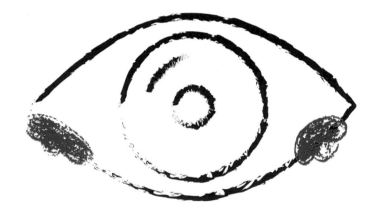

BEGINNING SCIENCE: GROSS BODY FUNTIONS

Abdo Kids Jumbo is an Imprint of Abdo Kids
abdobooks.com

**abdobooks.com**

Published by Abdo Kids, a division of ABDO, P.O. Box 398166, Minneapolis, Minnesota 55439.
Copyright © 2021 by Abdo Consulting Group, Inc. International copyrights reserved in all countries.
No part of this book may be reproduced in any form without written permission from the publisher.
Abdo Kids Jumbo™ is a trademark and logo of Abdo Kids.

Printed in the United States of America, North Mankato, Minnesota.

102020

012021

**THIS BOOK CONTAINS
RECYCLED MATERIALS**

Photo Credits: iStock, Science Source, Shutterstock

Production Contributors: Teddy Borth, Jennie Forsberg, Grace Hansen
Design Contributors: Dorothy Toth, Pakou Moua

Library of Congress Control Number: 2019956490

Publisher's Cataloging-in-Publication Data

Names: Hansen, Grace, author.

Title: Eye gunk / by Grace Hansen

Description: Minneapolis, Minnesota : Abdo Kids, 2021 | Series: Beginning science: gross body functions |
    Includes online resources and index.

Identifiers: ISBN 9781098202385 (lib. bdg.) | ISBN 9781644943854 (pbk.) | ISBN 9781098203368 (ebook)
    | ISBN 9781098203856 (Read-to-Me ebook)

Subjects: LCSH: Human body--Juvenile literature. | Mucus--Juvenile literature. | Eye--Care and hygiene—
    Juvenile literature. | Excretion--Juvenile literature. | Hygiene--Juvenile literature.

Classification: DDC 612--dc23

# Table of Contents

## Rheum Taking Up Room

Eye gunk can look and feel pretty gross. But it is there for important reasons!

5

Eye gunk is also known as **rheum**. Rheum is a collection of the things our eyes make and stuff that enters our eyes.

6

7

**Rheum** is mostly made up of the **mucus** produced by the **conjunctiva**. The conjunctiva coats the eyelids and the white part of the eyes.

rheum

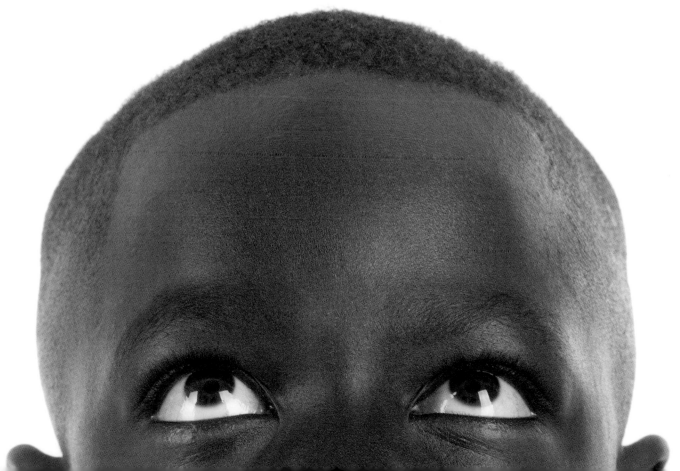

9

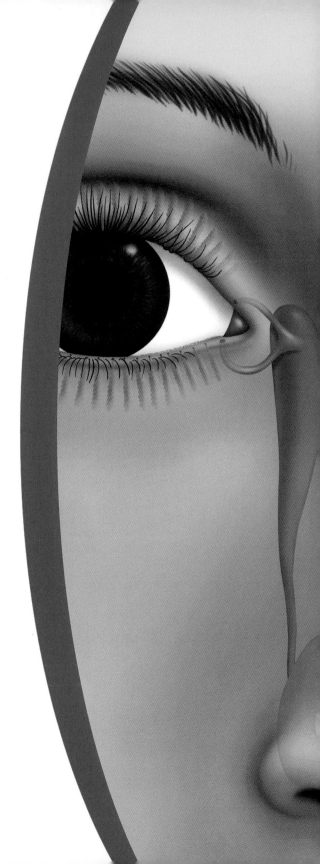

The eyes make **mucus** to protect themselves. Mucus catches and clears away things, like dirt, that enter the eyes.

10

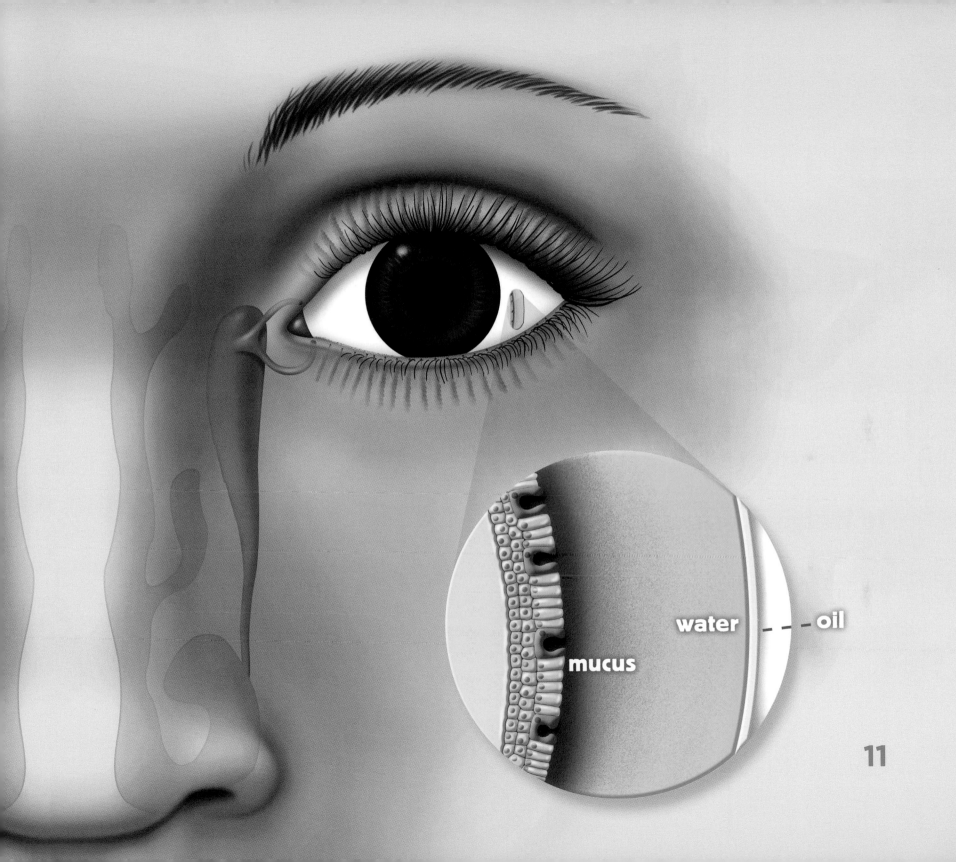

mucus

water

oil

11

## Making Meibum

Eyes also make an oily substance called **meibum**. It helps keep moisture from leaving the eyes.

12

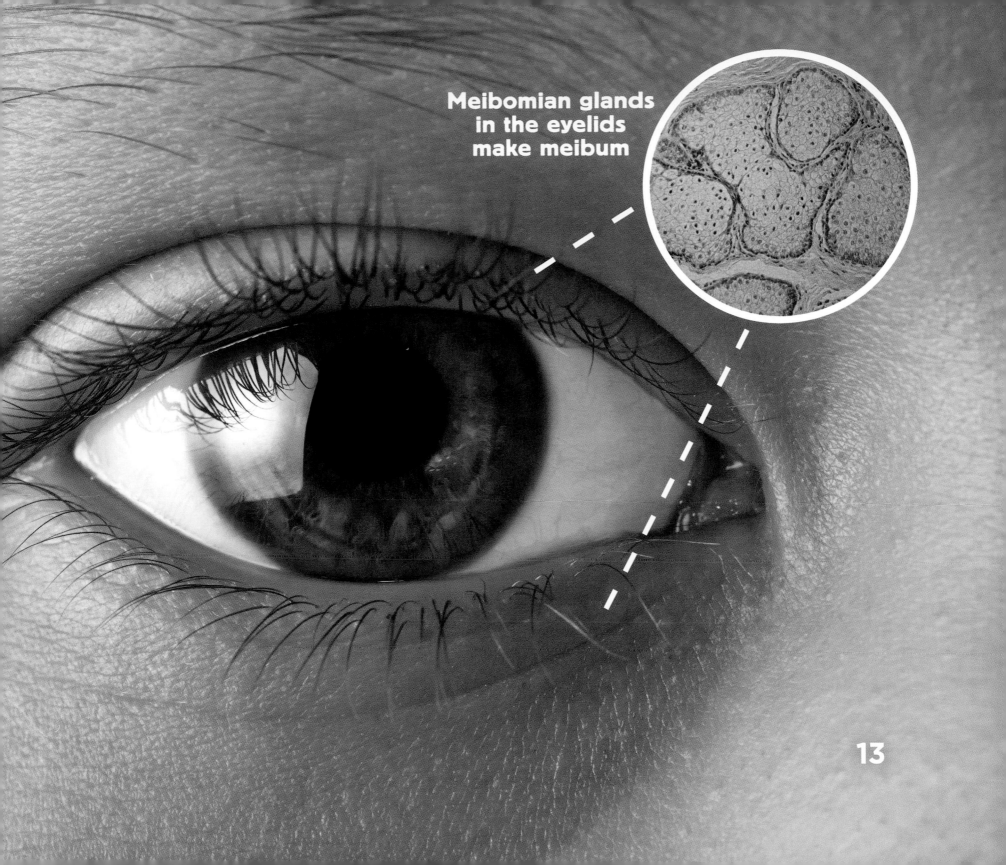

Meibomian glands
in the eyelids
make meibum

13

# Eye Issues

The eyelids clear away **mucus** and **meibum** with every blink. But we do not blink when we sleep. This allows **rheum** to build up.

14

This build up often gathers in the inner corners of the eyes. **Rheum** can also gather along the lids. Then it dries up.

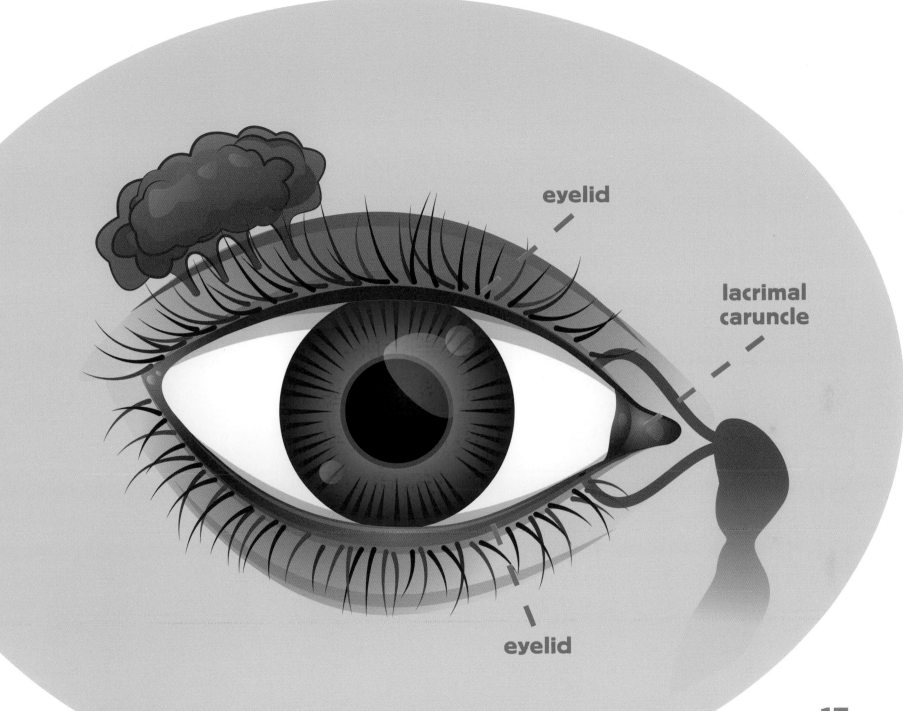

eyelid

lacrimal
caruncle

eyelid

17

It is easy to wash or wipe eye gunk away. Just be careful not to scratch your eye while doing it.

19

Sometimes eye gunk can be a problem. Our eyes can make too much of it. This can happen when our eyes are **irritated** by things like **allergies**.

21

# Let's Review!

- Eye gunk is mostly made up of mucus. The scientific word for eye gunk is rheum.

- The thin, watery mucus made by the conjunctiva protects the eyes. It catches and clears away anything that enters the eyes.

- Meibum helps keep eyes from drying out.

- When we blink, our eyelids clear away the things that make up rheum.

- When we sleep, our eyes stay closed. Our eyelids cannot clear things away. Rheum collects and hardens.

# Glossary

**allergy** – a condition in which a person's body has an unusual reaction to certain things.

**conjunctiva** – the mucous membrane that covers the front of the eye and lines the inside of the eyelids.

**irritated** – bothered or made red and inflamed.

**meibum** – made by the Meibomian glands that sit along the eyelids, an oily substance that keeps eyes healthy.

**mucus** – a slimy, slightly sticky material that coats and protects certain parts of the body.

**rheum** – a substance made up of mucus, meibum, and other things.

# Index

**Abdo Kids**
ONLINE
FREE! ONLINE MULTIMEDIA RESOURCES

Visit **abdokids.com** to access crafts, games, videos, and more!

Use Abdo Kids code
**BEK2385**
or scan this QR code!